Table of Contents:

Copyright © 2024 by Dr. ARUN MAJI
Table of Contents: 3
Preface: Does Poetry Heal?   5

Section 1: Tagore's Healing Poems with Annotations   7
    1. If No One Responds To Your Call   8
    2. Where The Mind Is Without Fear   9
    3. Leave This   11
    4. The Stream of Life   13
    4. Endless Time   14
    5. Let Me Not Forget   16
    6. Open the Doors, O Human   18
    7. O Lover, O Traveler of Great Journey   20
    8. The Paradox of Destruction: Commentary   22
    9. In the Face of Death   24
    10. Embracing Life's Duality: Commentary   26
    11. When the Time Comes   28
    12. Death, You Are Like My Beloved.   30
    13. Embracing Death as a Beloved: Commentary   31
    14. Where Does The Journey End   32
    15. Embracing the Uncertainty of the Journey; Commentary   33
    16. In the Daylight, Your Flute Played   35
    17. The Journey from External Seeking to Internal Fulfillment: Commentary   36
    18. When Darkness Fell   38
    19. Finding Light in Darkness: Commentary   39
    20. The Unfinished Song   41
    21. When I Hear My Name from Your Lips   44

22. The Power of Divine Recognition: Commentary	46
23. Did You Not Recognize Me?	48
24. Navigating Missed Opportunities and Longing: Commentary	50
25. The Day My Song Meets Yours	52
26. With Great Hope I Have Come	54
27. What Have You Done in the Illusion?	55
28. The Day Has Passed, Lord	57
29. I Am a Traveler	58
30. In Joy I Have Seen You	60
31. Eyes Cannot See You	62
32. I Will Not Tell You of My Sorrows	64
33. Forgive My Weariness, Lord	66
34. Through the Song	67
35. The Traveler Thought	68
36. One Silent Night	70
37. Play Me	72

Section 2: Healing and Tagore — 73

1. Why Does Poetry Heal	74
2. Healing Attributes of Humanity	77
3. Tagore and the Bhagavad Gita	83
3. Healing vs Personal Identity	86
4. Science vs Religion: Discord or Symphony?	88
5. Tagore as a Healer, Humanist, and Proponent of Human Identity	91
Author's Bio	94

Preface: Does Poetry Heal?

Welcome to the **world of healing through poetry.** "30 Jewels: Heal Through Tagore" explores the healing works of Nobel laureate poet Rabindranath Tagore.

But can poetry heal? Can the words of poets truly touch your soul and mend your spirit? The answer is a resounding yes.

But how does this work? Why do the verses of Tagore have such a profound impact on us? Because Tagore explored fundamental aspects of human existence that do not change with time or place. They still resonate with us as they did a hundred years ago.

Healing is a multidimensional process. While it's crucial to see doctors and seek professional advice for physical and mental health, exploring other avenues of healing can be equally important. Poetry is one such avenue.

Have you ever felt accompanied, supported, and guided by your mother or father? Did you feel secure and comforted while being with them? Yes, you did. Poetry can do the same thing for you.

Poetry serves as a mirror for self-reflection. It can help you see your own emotions more clearly. By reflecting on the themes and emotions in a poem, you can gain insights into your own life and emotions, fostering self-awareness and growth.

Poetry can diagnose your strengths and weaknesses, much like a doctor. Understanding your capabilities and areas for improvement enables you to address your flaws and leverage your strengths.

Gentle, comforting words can reduce stress and anxiety, creating a sense of well-being. Poetry can provide you with moral support and encouragement whenever you need it. **Inspirational verses can uplift your spirits, motivate you to persevere, and provide comfort during difficult times.**

Poetry offers hope and light in the darkest of times. It can **be a positive hiding place** from pain. Engaging with poetry can provide a temporary escape from life's challenges, allowing you to recover and recharge. Getting lost in **poetry is like surrogate meditation.** It calms you down and brings you serenity.

Tagore is a healer who heals our wounds through his poetry and song. Dive into this book now and discover how.

This book features:
- Selected poems by Tagore
- Annotations: "What does it mean?" and "How does it heal?" for each poem
- Discussion on Common Healing Attributes of Humans
- Step-by-Step Guidance to Heal

Who is this book for?
Anyone who is seeking healing and solace. But tell me, who isn't? We all have our wounds, we all crave healing each moment. So why don't you trust these healing words? Take a cup of tea and get lost on this journey.

Happy Healing!

Section 1: Tagore's Healing Poems with Annotations

1. If No One Responds To Your Call

If no one responds to your call,
Then walk alone.

If no one speaks,
Amidst the stormy winds,
Then walk alone.

If they do not come,
Facing the turbulent gales,
Then walk alone.

What Does It Mean?
This poem emphasizes the importance of individual courage and perseverance. It encourages us to continue our journey and stay true to our convictions, even if we find ourselves alone. Tagore is urging us to have the strength to walk our path, regardless of whether others join us or not.

How Does It Heal?
"Walk Alone" offers solace to those who feel isolated or unsupported. It empowers individuals to embrace their inner strength and resolve. By encouraging self-reliance and resilience, the poem serves as a reminder that we possess the courage to face challenges independently. This sense of

empowerment and self-assurance can be incredibly healing during times of loneliness or adversity.

2. Where The Mind Is Without Fear

Where the mind is without fear,
And the head is held high;

Where knowledge is free,
Where the world has not been broken up
Into fragments by narrow domestic walls;

Where words come out from the depth of truth;
Where tireless striving stretches its arms towards perfection;

Where the clear stream of reason has not lost its way
Into the dreary desert sand of dead habit;

Where the mind is led forward by thee
Into ever-widening thought and action—

Into that heaven of freedom, my Father, let my country awake.

What Does It Mean?
This poem envisions an ideal world where fear does not constrain the mind and where people hold their heads high with dignity. It calls for a society where knowledge is freely accessible, and divisions based on narrow domestic walls are

non-existent. Tagore emphasizes the importance of truth, continuous striving for perfection, and the supremacy of reason over blind habit. Ultimately, he prays for a nation awakened to freedom and progressive thought.

How Does It Heal?

"Where the Mind is Without Fear" instills hope and inspiration. It encourages us to envision a better, freer, and more enlightened world. By advocating for courage, dignity, and the pursuit of truth, the poem uplifts the reader's spirit. It serves as a beacon of hope for those feeling oppressed or constrained, offering a vision of a world where freedom and knowledge prevail. This inspirational message can bring healing by fostering a sense of purpose and optimism.

3. Leave This

Leave this chanting and singing and telling of beads!
Whom do you worship in this lonely dark corner of a temple with doors all shut?
Open your eyes and see your God is not before you!

He is there where the tiller is tilling the hard ground
and where the path-maker is breaking stones.
He is with them in the sun and in the shower,
and his garment is covered with dust.
Put off your holy mantle
and even like him come down on the dusty soil!

Deliverance? Where is this deliverance to be found?
Our master himself has joyfully taken upon him the bonds of creation;
He is bound with us all forever.

Come out of your meditations
and leave aside your flowers and incense!
What harm is there if your clothes become tattered and stained?
Meet him and stand by him in toil and in the sweat of your brow.

What Does It Mean?

In this poem, Tagore urges people to seek the divine not in secluded worship but in the everyday toil and struggles of life. He criticizes the act of worshiping in isolation and encourages people to find God among those who work hard in the fields and on the roads. The divine is present in the dust and sweat of everyday labor, not just in the confines of a temple.

How Does It Heal?

"Leave This" offers a powerful message of finding spirituality and divine presence in everyday life. It encourages us to step out of secluded practices and engage with the world around us. By recognizing the sacred in daily toil and human connections, we can find a deeper sense of purpose and fulfillment. This perspective fosters empathy, humility, and a greater appreciation for the shared human experience, leading to emotional and spiritual healing.

4. The Stream of Life

The same stream of life that runs through my veins night and day
runs through the world and dances in rhythmic measures.

It is the same life that shoots in joy
through the dust of the earth in numberless blades of grass
and breaks into tumultuous waves of leaves and flowers.

It is the same life
that is rocked in the ocean-cradle of birth and death,
in ebb and in flow.

I feel my limbs are made glorious by the touch of this world of life.
And my pride is from the life-throb of ages
dancing in my blood this moment.

What Does It Mean?
This poem celebrates the unity of life and the connection between the individual and the world. Tagore speaks of the same stream of life flowing through his veins and the world, creating a sense of oneness. He describes the joy and vitality that permeate nature and human existence, emphasizing the cyclical nature of life through birth and death.

How Does It Heal?

"The Stream of Life" offers a sense of interconnectedness and belonging. By recognizing the shared stream of life that runs through all living beings, we can find solace and strength in our connection to the world. The poem encourages us to embrace the vitality and joy of life, fostering a sense of unity and purpose. This perspective helps us appreciate the beauty of life and find comfort in the natural cycles of existence.

4. Endless Time

Time is endless in thy hands, my lord.
There is none to count thy minutes.

Days and nights pass and ages bloom and fade like flowers.
Thou knowest how to wait.

Thy centuries follow each other perfecting a small wild flower.

We have no time to lose,
and having no time we must scramble for our chances.
We are too poor to be late.

And thus it is that time goes by
while I give it to every querulous man who claims it,
and thine altar is empty of all offerings to the last.

At the end of the day I hasten in fear lest thy gate be shut;
but I find that yet there is time.

What Does It Mean?
This poem reflects on the concept of time and the divine's infinite patience. Tagore contrasts the eternal, unhurried nature of the divine with human beings' frantic scramble to make the most of their limited time. He acknowledges the

tendency to get caught up in daily demands, often neglecting what is truly important, only to realize that the divine always waits with open arms.

How Does It Heal?

"Endless Time" offers a comforting reminder of the divine's infinite patience and the boundless nature of time. It encourages us to pause and reflect on our priorities, recognizing that while we may feel rushed, the divine presence remains constant and patient. This perspective helps us find peace in the midst of our busy lives, encouraging us to focus on what truly matters and to trust in the divine's enduring presence.

5. Let Me Not Forget

If it is not my portion to meet thee in this life
then let me ever feel that I have missed thy sight—
let me not forget for a moment,
let me carry the pangs of this sorrow
in my dreams and in my wakeful hours.

As my days pass in the crowded market of this world
and my hands grow full with the daily profits,
let me ever feel that I have gained nothing—
let me not forget for a moment,
let me carry the pangs of this sorrow
in my dreams and in my wakeful hours.

When I sit by the roadside, tired and panting,
when I spread my bed low in the dust,
let me ever feel that the long journey is still before me—
let me not forget for a moment,
let me carry the pangs of this sorrow
in my dreams and in my wakeful hours.

When my rooms have been decked out
and the flutes sound and the laughter there is loud,
let me ever feel that I have not invited thee to my house—
let me not forget for a moment,
let me carry the pangs of this sorrow

in my dreams and in my wakeful hours.

What Does It Mean?

This poem expresses a deep yearning for divine connection and the pain of feeling its absence. Tagore speaks of carrying the sorrow of not meeting the divine in this life as a constant reminder. He contrasts the busyness and material gains of daily life with the profound sense of loss for not having achieved spiritual fulfillment. The poem emphasizes the importance of this longing, keeping the desire for divine connection alive through all life's activities and moments.

How Does It Heal?

"Let Me Not Forget" offers a poignant reflection on the importance of spiritual longing and the search for deeper meaning. It reassures us that it is natural to feel a sense of sorrow for not achieving spiritual fulfillment. By keeping this longing alive, the poem encourages a continuous search for deeper connection and purpose. This perspective fosters resilience, as it motivates us to look beyond material gains and daily routines, seeking a higher purpose and spiritual fulfillment.

6. Open the Doors, O Human

Open the doors, O human,
Do not stay hidden away--
Bring out whatever you have,
All must be given and settled.
No one should sleep anymore.
Open your heart
And fill the vessel of offering.
O humble soul, why stay attached to things
You never truly possess?

On the path of ascension, I hear a voice,
"Fear not, O fear not--
He who sacrifices his life
Knows no decay, knows no end."
O divine Rudra, tell me how to sing
Your song, my Lord--
I will beat the drum of my heart
To the rhythm of death's dance,
I will gather my sorrow
To prepare your offering.
Dawn has come, a new dawn.
Shiva, the destroyer of darkness,
Has laughed his sacred laugh!
He who has awakened today
Is filled with immense joy.

What Does It Mean?

This poem is a call to awaken and embrace the dawn of a new day. Tagore urges people to open their doors, let go of hidden fears, and share everything they have. It is a plea to reject false attachments and to give completely. The poem speaks of a voice encouraging bravery and selflessness, assuring that those who give their all will never perish. The imagery of Rudra (a form of Shiva) and the drum of the heart emphasizes a powerful, transformative journey towards enlightenment and joy.

How Does It Heal?

"Open the Doors, O Human" encourages awakening and the shedding of fears and attachments. It speaks to the power of selflessness and the joy that comes from true awakening. By urging individuals to embrace their inner strength and face life's challenges with courage, the poem provides a sense of liberation and empowerment. This message of fearless giving and profound joy can be deeply healing, helping individuals to transcend their limitations and find inner peace and happiness.

7. O Lover, O Traveler of Great Journey

O lover, O traveler of great journey,
In separation, you unite.
In destruction, you create.
Come, everyone,
To the grand festival of the song of destruction.

Wind swirls, storm blows,
The sky echoes the roar of the storm,
Raising fear--
In the dance of Rudra, the destroyer and the terminator,
All rhythms cease and bonds are severed.
Yet in that destruction, creation begins.
In the hearts of those mad for liberation,
The fire of love's devotion will burn.

O lover, O traveler of great journey,
When all hope fades away,
When beyond hope stands the true world--
Silence speaks the truth.
Come, everyone,
To the grand festival of the song of destruction.

What Does It Mean?
This poem speaks to the transformative power of separation and destruction. Tagore portrays the journey of the lover and

the traveler as one where unity is found in separation and creation arises from destruction. The chaotic dance of Rudra symbolizes the fierce forces that end old cycles and initiate new beginnings. The poem emphasizes that true liberation and profound devotion emerge from embracing this transformative process.

How Does It Heal?
"O Lover, O Traveler of Great Journey" offers a perspective that finds hope and renewal in the face of destruction and separation. It reassures that within chaos lies the seed of creation and within despair, the spark of liberation. By accepting the cycles of ending and beginning, individuals can find peace and strength.

8. The Paradox of Destruction: Commentary

In the preceding poems, Tagore captures the profound paradox of destruction. He suggests that what we see is not always what it is. Within destruction hides creation; within separation hides union. These seemingly opposite forces are, in fact, two sides of the same coin, each containing the seed of the other.

Tagore implicitly suggests the duality of nature—that creation and destruction, positive and negative, light and shadow—are interconnected. They can flip at any moment, existing in a delicate balance and rhythm throughout life. This understanding can be profoundly healing, offering a new perspective on the challenges we face.

Embracing the Duality
In "Open the Doors, O Human," Tagore calls for an awakening, urging us to open our hearts and let go of false attachments. He speaks of a transformative journey where fear and doubt are left behind. The poem reassures us that through the chaos and breaking of old bonds, a deeper union and completeness can be found. This is a powerful message of hope and resilience.

In "O Lover, O Traveler of Great Journey," Tagore further explores this theme. He portrays the journey of the lover and the traveler as one where unity is found in separation and creation arises from destruction. The chaotic dance of Rudra symbolizes the fierce forces that end old cycles and initiate new beginnings. The poem emphasizes that true liberation and profound devotion emerge from embracing this transformative process.

The Healing Power of Understanding
Understanding the paradox of destruction is deeply healing. It teaches us not to fear when we face negativity in life. When we encounter destruction, it is not the end, but a precursor to new beginnings. When we experience separation, it is not permanent, but a step towards a deeper connection. This perspective helps us navigate life's challenges with greater resilience and inner peace.

Life is full of cycles—birth and death, joy and sorrow, creation and destruction. By embracing this duality, we learn to see beyond the immediate pain and chaos. We recognize that every end carries the promise of a new beginning. This understanding fosters a sense of hope and strength, encouraging us to persevere through difficult times.

A Message of Resilience
So, when you encounter the storms of life, remember Tagore's wisdom. Do not fear the darkness, for it is where the light is born. Do not despair in destruction, for it is the

seed of creation. Embrace the duality of existence, and find strength in the rhythm of life's cycles. This perspective will guide you through the toughest times, helping you emerge stronger and more connected to the world around you.

9. In the Face of Death

Abandoning me in the face of death,
Go far away,
Yet return again, drawn by heartache.

Across the edge of darkness and light,
I wander back and forth,
Losing myself only to find myself again,
Swinging between the eternal rhythm of loss and find.

Every melody, I believe, will play in my soul--
Sometimes in fear, sometimes in triumph,
Sometimes in shame, sometimes in pride.

Separation will tune, so keep me distant,
Union will play the flute, so pull me close.

No matter if you go or stay,
Life will play music anyway.
Life does so,
But do we truly realize this?

What Does It Mean?
This poem delves into the duality of life and death, separation and union. Tagore speaks of the paradox of being abandoned in the face of death, yet being drawn back

by the pain of separation. He portrays the journey between darkness and light as an eternal rhythm, a constant search for self through loss and discovery. The poem suggests that every emotion—fear, triumph, shame, pride—contributes to the melody of life. In separation, a poignant tune plays, while in union, a joyful flute sings. The concluding lines reflect on the inevitability of life's music, urging us to recognize and understand this profound truth.

How Does It Heal?

"In the Face of Death" offers a perspective on the inherent duality of existence. It reassures us that separation and union are both essential parts of life's rhythm. By recognizing that every emotion and experience contributes to the greater symphony of life, we can find peace in both joy and sorrow. The poem's message encourages us to embrace the ebb and flow of life, understanding that pain and pleasure, loss and gain, are intertwined. This acceptance fosters resilience and inner harmony, helping us navigate life's challenges with grace.

10. Embracing Life's Duality: Commentary

In the preceding poem, Tagore again captures the paradoxical nature of existence. He highlights that separation and union, darkness and light, fear and triumph, are all part of life's intricate dance. This duality is not a contradiction but a profound truth that can bring healing and inspiration.

The Eternal Rhythm
Tagore illustrates the eternal rhythm of life through the metaphor of crossing the edge of darkness and light. This constant movement, losing oneself to find oneself, symbolizes the journey of self-discovery and growth. By accepting that life is a series of such crossings, we can find solace in the midst of uncertainty.

The Symphony of Emotions
The poem emphasizes that every emotion plays a role in the symphony of life. Fear, triumph, shame, and pride are all notes that create a complete and beautiful melody. This perspective helps us appreciate the full range of our experiences, understanding that each one is valuable and necessary for our growth.

Finding Peace in Duality

Tagore's insight into the duality of life teaches us not to fear separation or death, for they are integral to the cycle of existence. Separation and pain are not ends in themselves but parts of a larger process that includes union and joy. By embracing this duality, we can find peace and strength, knowing that every end is a new beginning.

A Message of Resilience

When we understand that separation and union are intertwined, we can face life's challenges with greater courage and acceptance.

So, when you encounter moments of separation or fear, remember Tagore's wisdom. Embrace the full range of your emotions and experiences, knowing that they all contribute to the rich tapestry of life. Find strength in the duality of existence, and let it guide you towards inner peace and resilience.

11. When the Time Comes

When the time comes,
I shall depart.

Yet how much I loved this light and dark,
Playing in the vast sky.
Days passed in a myriad of things,
In joy and sorrow,
Shame and pride.

For a long time, I tried hard to repay my debts,
Yet sometimes, I was indifferent, forgetting everything.
Sometimes I played, floating my boat on the stream,
Spending many moments in a trance.

Life was not in vain; it was covered with fruits and flowers.
If anything remains, who will take it?
All give and take will be settled,
My heart will be relieved of burdens.
I will go with a smiling face—
Happy and serene.

What Does It Mean?
This poem reflects on the inevitability of departure and the acceptance of life's journey. Tagore speaks of his deep affection for the interplay of light and dark in the world and

the many ways he has experienced life. He acknowledges the joy and sorrow, pride and shame, and the efforts to repay debts, sometimes failing and sometimes succeeding. He reminisces about the carefree moments spent playing and floating on life's stream. Tagore concludes that life was not in vain, and all remaining burdens will be lifted as he departs silently with a smile.

How Does It Heal?

"When the Time Comes" offers a perspective on accepting the end of life's journey with grace and peace. It reassures us that life, with all its light and dark moments, is meaningful and beautiful. By reflecting on both the joys and struggles, the poem encourages a sense of fulfillment and acceptance. The message that all debts and burdens will be settled provides comfort, suggesting that we can leave this world with a light heart and a smiling face. This perspective helps us embrace the end of life with dignity and serenity, finding peace in the inevitability of departure.

12. Death, You Are Like My Beloved.

Death, you are like my beloved.
Your complexion is dark as clouds, your hair like a stormy sky,
With hands of red lotus and lips crimson,
You relieve the pain with your merciful touch,
And transform death into nectar.

Agonized like Radha, fragile and yearning,
Tears continuously stream from my eyes--
You are my Krishna, you are my companion,
You are the one to remove my pain.
Death, come to me, come.

What Does It Mean?
This poem portrays death not as an enemy, but as a beloved and compassionate entity. Tagore likens death to Krishna, the divine lover, and sees it as a source of relief and transformation. The imagery of dark clouds, stormy hair, and crimson lips conveys a powerful, yet soothing presence. The reference to Radha's yearning symbolizes the soul's longing for liberation and union with the divine. Tagore calls for death to come and relieve his pain, transforming the fear of death into a serene acceptance.

How Does It Heal?

"Death, You Are My Beloved" offers a comforting and transformative perspective on death. By depicting death as a compassionate and beloved figure, the poem alleviates the fear and dread often associated with it. Tagore's imagery of death as Krishna, the divine lover, reassures us that death is a part of the divine plan, a means to ultimate liberation and peace. This acceptance helps us embrace the end of life with serenity and trust, finding solace in the inevitable transition.

13. Embracing Death as a Beloved: Commentary

In this poem, Tagore captures a profound and compassionate perspective on death. He presents death not as a fearsome end, but as a beloved companion that brings relief and transformation.

The Compassionate Face of Death
Tagore portrays death with the loving attributes of Krishna, depicting it as a compassionate and merciful force. This imagery transforms the fear of death into a comforting presence, helping us see it as a natural and divine part of life's journey.

The Yearning for Liberation
The poem references Radha's yearning for Krishna, symbolizing the soul's longing for liberation and union with the divine. This longing is met with the promise of relief and transformation through death, providing a sense of peace and acceptance.

Transforming Fear into Acceptance
By likening death to a beloved figure, Tagore alleviates the fear and dread associated with it. This perspective encourages us to see death as a transition to a higher state of being, a means to ultimate liberation. Understanding death

as a compassionate force helps us face it with serenity and trust, fostering a deeper sense of peace.

A Message of Serenity and Trust

The poem's message encourages us to embrace death with serenity and trust. It reassures us that death is not an end, but a transformation that brings relief and peace. By accepting death as a beloved companion, we can navigate the end of life with grace and calm, finding solace in the inevitable transition.

So, when you reflect on the end of life, remember Tagore's wisdom. Embrace death as a compassionate and beloved force, and find peace in the understanding that it is a part of the divine plan. This perspective will guide you towards a serene and dignified acceptance of life's end.

14. Where Does The Journey End

Where does the journey end? Where?
What lies at the end?
Where do all these desires and efforts merge?
Tears flow like a flood, darkness lies ahead,
There is a shore, there is one—yet where?
I wonder in my mind,
All in the quest for mirages.
But now I realize there is no end to thirst.
It scares me--
A broken dream, a torn sail, pain drifts into the unknown.

What Does It Mean?

This poem reflects on the uncertainty and endless pursuit of desires and efforts. Tagore questions the ultimate destination of life's journey, pondering where all the aspirations and struggles lead. The imagery of tears flowing like a flood and dense darkness ahead symbolizes the turmoil and uncertainties faced along the way. The quest for a distant shore, possibly a metaphor for ultimate fulfillment or peace, seems elusive, much like a mirage. The realization that thirst, or longing, never truly ends brings a sense of fear and discomfort, symbolized by a broken dream and a torn sail drifting aimlessly.

How Does It Heal?

"Where Does the Journey End?" offers a contemplative perspective on the human condition. It acknowledges the endless nature of desires and the uncertainties of life's journey, encouraging introspection. By recognizing that the search for fulfillment often leads to more longing, the poem invites us to find peace in the journey itself rather than in the elusive destination. This acceptance helps us embrace life's uncertainties with a sense of calm and resilience, understanding that the quest itself holds value and meaning.

15. Embracing the Uncertainty of the Journey; Commentary

In this poem, Tagore captures the essence of the human quest for meaning and fulfillment. He reflects on the endless pursuit of desires and the uncertainties of life's journey.

The Endless Pursuit
Tagore questions where the journey ends and where all desires and efforts merge. This reflection highlights the perpetual nature of human longing and the elusive quest for ultimate fulfillment. By acknowledging the endless pursuit, the poem invites us to find value in the journey itself.

The Turmoil and Darkness
The imagery of tears flowing like a flood and dense darkness ahead symbolizes the challenges and uncertainties we face. Tagore's portrayal of these elements reflects the turmoil inherent in the human experience. Recognizing these challenges helps us develop resilience and a deeper understanding of life's complexities.

The Elusive Shore
The poem speaks of a distant shore, representing ultimate fulfillment or peace, which seems elusive like a mirage. This metaphor emphasizes the idea that true fulfillment often lies beyond our reach. By accepting this, we can shift our focus

from the destination to the journey, finding peace in the present moment.

Finding Peace in the Journey
Tagore's realization that there is no end to thirst brings a sense of fear and discomfort. However, this recognition also offers a path to healing. By understanding that the quest for fulfillment is continuous, we can embrace the journey with a sense of calm and acceptance. This perspective helps us navigate life's uncertainties with grace, finding meaning and value in the journey itself.

A Message of Resilience and Acceptance
The poem's message encourages us to embrace the uncertainties of life's journey. It reassures us that the search for fulfillment is an integral part of the human experience. By accepting the endless nature of desires and finding peace in the journey, we can cultivate resilience and a deeper sense of fulfillment.

Embrace the uncertainties and endless pursuits, and find peace in the present moment. This perspective will guide you towards a resilient and accepting approach to life's journey.

16. In the Daylight, Your Flute Played

In the daylight, your flute played many melodies—
Your song reached my soul, yet you remained distant.
I asked every traveler, "Who played this flute?"
—They misled me with many names,
and I wandered to many doors.

Now the sun is setting,
the tired day closes its eyes—
If you keep wandering,
I will perish in a false search.
Why wander outside?
Come within me,
and take your seat—
Play your flute here,
In the innermost chamber of my soul.

What Does It Mean?
This poem speaks of the elusive nature of the divine or the beloved, symbolized by the flute's melody. In the bright daylight, the enchanting music touches the poet's soul, yet the source remains distant. The poet's quest to find the flutist leads to misdirection and wandering. As the day ends and the sun sets, the poet recognizes the futility of seeking externally. Instead, he invites the divine to settle within, to

42

play the flute in the innermost chamber of his soul, signifying a deeper, internal connection.

How Does It Heal?
"In the Daylight, Your Flute Played" offers a healing message about the shift from external search to internal realization. It reassures that true connection and fulfillment are found within ourselves. By inviting the divine or the beloved to reside in the innermost part of our being, the poem encourages introspection and inner peace. This shift from external seeking to internal fulfillment fosters a deeper sense of serenity and connection, helping us find peace and joy within.

17. The Journey from External Seeking to Internal Fulfillment: Commentary

In this poem, Tagore captures the essence of the quest for the divine or the beloved, illustrating the journey from external seeking to internal fulfillment.

The Elusive Melody
Tagore describes the enchanting melodies of the flute heard in the daylight, symbolizing the divine or the beloved's presence. The music touches the poet's soul, yet the source remains distant, leading to a quest to identify and find the flutist. This represents the human tendency to seek fulfillment and connection outside of ourselves.

The Misleading Quest
The poet's journey to find the flutist through questioning travelers and wandering to many doors illustrates the often misleading and futile nature of external searches. This misdirection emphasizes the challenges and frustrations of seeking fulfillment in the external world.

The Internal Realization
As the day ends and the sun sets, the poet realizes the futility of the external quest. The recognition that true connection lies within marks a significant shift in understanding. By inviting the divine to settle within and play the flute in the

innermost chamber of his soul, the poet embraces the internal source of fulfillment and peace.

Finding Peace Within

Tagore's invitation to the divine to reside within the innermost chamber of the soul highlights the importance of introspection and internal connection. This shift from external seeking to internal realization fosters a deeper sense of serenity and fulfillment. By recognizing that true peace and joy come from within, we can navigate life with a greater sense of inner calm and connection.

A Message of Inner Fulfillment

The poem's message encourages us to shift our focus from external searches to internal realization. It reassures us that true fulfillment and connection are found within ourselves. By embracing this internal source of peace and joy, we can cultivate a deeper sense of serenity and fulfillment, helping us navigate life's challenges with grace and inner strength.

18. When Darkness Fell

Because the darkness fell,
Light kindled in my home.
What I forgot by day, I found by night—
I discovered whose play stirs my heart.
In my sleepless forest,
Birdsong echoed every moment.
When all sounds fell silent,
Spring's breeze roused me with rustling leaves.

What Does It Mean?

This poem reflects the paradox that light often emerges from darkness. Tagore speaks of finding illumination in times of darkness, symbolizing deeper understanding and awareness that comes in challenging times. By night, what was forgotten during the day is rediscovered, and the poet realizes the divine play that stirs his heart. The sleepless forest and the birdsong signify the moments of awakening and realization. As all sounds fall silent, the gentle breeze of spring revives the poet, symbolizing hope and renewal.

How Does It Heal?

"When Darkness Fell" offers a comforting message that light and understanding can emerge from darkness and challenges. It reassures us that difficult times often lead to deeper insights and renewed awareness. By embracing the darkness, we can find the light within and rediscover what truly matters. The poem encourages us to find moments of awakening and renewal, symbolized by the birdsong and spring breeze, fostering hope and resilience.

19. Finding Light in Darkness: Commentary

In this poem, Tagore captures the essence of discovering light and understanding in times of darkness. He illustrates how challenges and difficulties can lead to deeper insights and renewal.

The Emergence of Light

Tagore begins with the idea that light kindles when darkness falls. This symbolizes the emergence of understanding and awareness in challenging times. It reassures us that even in the darkest moments, there is the potential for illumination and growth.

Rediscovery and Realization

The poet speaks of rediscovering what was forgotten during the day by night, highlighting the paradox that sometimes, deeper understanding comes in moments of reflection and stillness. Tagore realizes the divine play that stirs his heart, symbolizing a profound connection to the inner self and the divine.

Awakening and Renewal

The sleepless forest and the birdsong signify moments of awakening and realization. These moments occur even in times of stillness and silence, offering glimpses of hope and renewal. The gentle breeze of spring rousing the poet with rustling leaves symbolizes the natural cycle of renewal and the promise of new beginnings.

Embracing Challenges

Tagore's message encourages us to embrace challenges and difficult times as opportunities for growth and understanding. By finding light in darkness and moments of awakening in stillness, we can navigate life's challenges with resilience and hope. This perspective helps us appreciate the value of both light and darkness in our journey.

A Message of Hope and Resilience

The poem's message is one of hope and resilience. It reassures us that light and understanding can emerge from darkness, and moments of awakening can occur even in stillness. By embracing the duality of light and darkness, we can find deeper insights and renewal, fostering a sense of inner peace and strength.

Embrace the potential for light and understanding within the darkness, and find moments of awakening and renewal. This perspective will guide you towards a resilient and hopeful approach to life's journey.

20. The Unfinished Song

The song I came to sing
remains unsung to this day.
I have spent my days in stringing
and in unstringing my instrument.

The time has not come true,
the words have not been rightly set;
only there is the agony
of wishing in my heart.

I have not seen his face,
nor have I listened to his voice;
only I have heard his gentle footsteps
from the road before my house.

But the lamp has not been lit
and I cannot ask him into my house;
I live in the hope of meeting with him,
but this meeting is not yet.

What Does It Mean?
This poem reflects the feeling of unfulfilled purpose and the yearning for a deeper connection with the divine. Tagore speaks of a song that remains unsung, symbolizing a mission or calling that has yet to be realized. The preparation—

stringing and unstringing the instrument—represents the effort and struggle involved in trying to fulfill this purpose. The poet hears the divine presence through gentle footsteps, yet the full encounter remains elusive. The unlit lamp signifies the poet's readiness and anticipation, but also the incomplete state of readiness to fully receive the divine.

How Does It Heal?

"The Unfinished Song" offers a poignant reflection on the universal experience of longing and the pursuit of one's purpose. It reassures us that feeling unfulfilled or waiting for the right moment is a common part of the human journey. By acknowledging this yearning and the efforts we put into preparation, the poem provides comfort and validation. It encourages patience and faith, reminding us that the journey itself holds value and that the awaited moment of fulfillment will come in its own time.

Annotations

The Unsung Song

The unsung song symbolizes unfulfilled dreams and aspirations. Tagore's admission of spending days in preparation—stringing and unstringing his instrument—reflects the continuous effort and the sense of incompletion many of us feel in our pursuits. This recognition validates our own experiences of struggle and preparation, offering solace in knowing that we are not alone in this journey.

The Agony of Wishing

The poet speaks of the "agony of wishing," capturing the deep yearning for fulfillment. This longing is a powerful emotional experience that drives us to keep striving. Tagore's expression of this agony resonates with readers, offering a sense of empathy and shared human experience. It reassures us that our desires and efforts, even when unfulfilled, are meaningful.

Gentle Footsteps

Hearing the "gentle footsteps" of the divine presence suggests that while the full encounter with the divine has not occurred, there are signs and moments of connection. This partial experience encourages us to remain attentive and open to the subtle signs of progress and connection in our own lives. It fosters a sense of hope and anticipation for the eventual realization of our goals.

The Unlit Lamp

The unlit lamp symbolizes readiness and the anticipation of fulfillment. Tagore's admission that he cannot yet invite the divine presence into his home because the lamp is unlit speaks to the feeling of incompleteness. This metaphor encourages us to continue preparing and nurturing our readiness, trusting that the right moment will come. It emphasizes the importance of patience and ongoing effort.

Living in Hope

The poet lives in the hope of meeting the divine, highlighting the role of hope in sustaining us through periods of waiting and preparation. This message is particularly healing, as it encourages us to maintain our faith and optimism even when our efforts seem unfulfilled. Hope becomes a guiding light, helping us navigate the uncertainties and delays in our journey.

Conclusion

"The Unfinished Song" beautifully captures the universal experience of longing and the pursuit of unfulfilled dreams. It encourages us to embrace our efforts, remain patient, and hold on to hope, trusting that the moment of fulfillment will come in its own time.

21. When I Hear My Name from Your Lips

When I hear my name from your lips, I burst into song—
"I am here, I am here."
In that very song, the mist of oblivion lifts,
I live, I live.

When you look at me in the nameless abode of the unspoken,
Light ignites—
The lifeless awakens, still snow melts,
In a dance of celebration.

With silent steps, dawn stands alone at the door of the world's slumber,
Calling out behind the veil of the crimson sky.
Immediately, morning emerges with its lyre in hand,
Filling the void with song;
Spreading its wealth with open hands across the sky,
It knows no fatigue.

What Does It Mean?
This poem speaks to the profound impact of divine recognition and connection. When the poet hears his name called by the divine, it evokes a powerful response, lifting him from oblivion and affirming his existence. The divine gaze in the nameless, unspoken realms brings light,

awakening, and transformation. The imagery of dawn standing at the door of slumber, calling out, and the morning emerging with a lyre symbolizes the arrival of enlightenment and inspiration, filling the void with song and spreading abundance tirelessly.

How Does It Heal?
"When I Hear My Name from Your Lips" offers a message of profound affirmation and awakening. The recognition by the divine and the subsequent transformation symbolize the power of divine connection to lift us from oblivion and affirm our existence. The poem reassures us that we are seen and valued by the divine, bringing light and awakening into our lives. This connection fosters a sense of purpose, inspiration, and resilience, helping us navigate life with a renewed sense of inner strength and joy.

22. The Power of Divine Recognition: Commentary

In this poem, Tagore captures the essence of divine recognition and its transformative impact on the human soul.

The Affirmation of Existence
Tagore begins with the powerful moment when the divine calls his name, leading to a burst of song and a profound affirmation of existence. This symbolizes the healing power of being recognized and valued by the divine, lifting us from the mist of oblivion and bringing us to life.

Awakening and Transformation
The divine gaze in the nameless abode of the unspoken ignites light and awakens the lifeless, symbolized by melting snow and the dance of celebration. This transformation reflects the profound impact of divine connection, bringing enlightenment and renewal.

The Arrival of Dawn
The imagery of dawn standing at the door of slumber, calling out, and the morning emerging with a lyre symbolizes the arrival of enlightenment and inspiration. This new beginning fills the void with song and spreads abundance tirelessly, representing the boundless energy and generosity of the divine.

Finding Purpose and Joy

Tagore's message encourages us to recognize the power of divine connection in affirming our existence and bringing light into our lives. By embracing this connection, we can find purpose, inspiration, and resilience. This understanding helps us navigate life's challenges with a renewed sense of inner strength and joy.

A Message of Divine Connection

The poem's message reassures us of the profound impact of divine recognition and connection. It affirms that we are seen and valued by the divine, bringing light and transformation into our lives. By embracing this connection, we can cultivate a deeper sense of purpose, inspiration, and resilience, helping us navigate life with a sense of joy and fulfillment.

So, when you reflect on your connection to the divine, remember Tagore's wisdom. Embrace the power of divine recognition and let it bring light and awakening into your life. This perspective will guide you towards a fulfilling and joyful journey through life.

23. Did You Not Recognize Me?

Did you not recognize me?
In the corner, without a lamp, I stood lost in thought,
You passed by without seeing anyone.

Had you come to my door, it would have opened with a touch—
But my boat of fortune
Was halted by this small barrier.

On a stormy night, I counted the hours.
Alas, I did not hear, I did not hear the sound of your chariot,
The sound of your chariot.

In the rumbling thunder, I trembled,
Holding my heart tightly,
Lightning blazed in the sky,
Writing a curse.

What Does It Mean?
This poem speaks of missed recognition and lost opportunities. Tagore describes standing unnoticed in a dark corner, symbolizing moments of being overlooked or forgotten. He reflects on how his fortune could have changed with just a touch, but it was halted by a small barrier. The

stormy night and the counting of hours represent waiting and longing. The missed sound of the divine chariot signifies missed opportunities for connection and recognition. The rumbling thunder and blazing lightning depict the intense emotions and perceived curses of those moments.

How Does It Heal?

"Did You Not Recognize Me?" offers a poignant reflection on the feelings of being overlooked and the pain of missed opportunities. By expressing these emotions, the poem validates the experience of being unseen and the longing for connection. It reassures that these moments of pain and longing are part of the human experience. By acknowledging these feelings, we can begin to heal and find solace in the understanding that recognition and connection may come at unexpected times. This perspective fosters resilience and acceptance, helping us navigate the complexities of life with a sense of inner strength and hope.

24. Navigating Missed Opportunities and Longing: Commentary

In this poem, Tagore captures the essence of missed recognition and the longing for connection, illustrating the pain and resilience that come with these experiences.

The Pain of Being Overlooked
Tagore begins with the experience of standing unnoticed in a dark corner, symbolizing moments of being overlooked or forgotten. This imagery conveys the deep pain and isolation that come with feeling unseen.

Missed Opportunities
The poet reflects on how his fortune could have changed with just a touch, but was halted by a small barrier. This highlights the frustration and sorrow of missed opportunities and the impact of seemingly minor obstacles on our paths.

The Stormy Night of Longing
The stormy night and the counting of hours represent the intense longing and waiting for recognition and connection. The missed sound of the divine chariot signifies the pain of missed opportunities for meaningful connection.

Intense Emotions and Healing

The rumbling thunder and blazing lightning depict the intense emotions and perceived curses of those moments. By expressing these emotions, the poem validates the pain and longing, offering a path to healing. Acknowledging these feelings helps us navigate the complexities of life with resilience and acceptance.

A Message of Resilience and Hope

Tagore's message encourages us to recognize and validate our feelings of being overlooked and the pain of missed opportunities. It reassures us that these experiences are part of the human journey. By acknowledging and expressing these emotions, we can find solace and begin to heal. This perspective fosters resilience and hope, helping us navigate life's challenges with inner strength.

So, when you reflect on moments of being overlooked or missed opportunities, remember Tagore's wisdom. Acknowledge your feelings and find solace in the understanding that recognition and connection may come at unexpected times.

25. The Day My Song Meets Yours

The day my song merges with the rhythm of your melody,
I will find the shore of liberation through the music of my soul.

On that day, I will understand that there are no bindings of matter,
In the emptiness, your lyre's vibration will take shape—
All burdens will fall away, all cries will cease,
I will lose myself in the rhythm and the beat,
My restless thoughts will find peace in the petals of the cosmic song.

I will surrender all my joys, sorrows, hopes, and despair
To the strings of your lyre—
They will take the form of a song, and I will humbly listen,
Bowing my head.

I will see where rainbows suddenly appear,
Where the dawn's shawl flutters on the horizon's edge,
Where the fragrance of wayward flowers rushes at noon—
On the wings of birds flying home,
Where the evening sky bids farewell to the day.

What Does It Mean?

This poem speaks to the profound connection between the individual soul and the divine through the medium of music. Tagore envisions a moment when his song merges perfectly with the divine melody, leading to a state of liberation and peace. The merging of the songs symbolizes the dissolution of all worldly bonds and the attainment of a harmonious state where burdens and sorrows vanish. The imagery of rainbows, dawn, and birds returning home evokes a sense of beauty, tranquility, and the cyclical nature of life.

How Does It Heal?

"The Day My Song Meets Yours" offers a vision of ultimate harmony and liberation. It reassures us that through a deep connection with the divine, symbolized by the merging of songs, we can find peace and freedom from worldly burdens. The poem encourages us to seek this divine connection within ourselves, promising that it will bring clarity and tranquility. By envisioning the beautiful imagery of nature and the cosmos, the poem fosters a sense of calm and inner peace, helping us navigate life's challenges with a serene and hopeful outlook.

26. With Great Hope I Have Come

With great hope I have come,
Please call me close,
Do not turn me away, Mother.

The destitute and humble have no one who cares for them,
But I know you will keep them.
I desire nothing else,
Just to sit at your feet.
I desire nothing else,
Just to call you Mother.

If you do not keep me,
where will I find a home?
Where will I wander, crying and crying—
In that dark, dense, and deep night?

What Does It Mean?
This poem expresses a deep longing for acceptance and refuge with a maternal figure, symbolizing a divine or spiritual entity. The poet approaches with great hope, seeking closeness and reassurance from the Mother. The destitute and humble, who have no one else to care for them, find solace in her presence. The poet desires nothing more than to sit at her feet and call her Mother. If she does not

accept him, he feels there is no place left to go, symbolizing the sense of despair and lostness without spiritual refuge.

How Does It Heal?

"With Great Hope I Have Come" offers a comforting message of seeking and finding solace in a maternal, divine presence. It reassures us that there is a place where even the destitute and humble are cared for and loved. By expressing this deep longing and the fear of being turned away, the poem validates feelings of vulnerability and the need for acceptance. It encourages us to seek spiritual refuge and find peace in the maternal embrace of the divine, fostering a sense of belonging, comfort, and inner strength.

27. What Have You Done in the Illusion?

What have you done in the illusion?
You left home and wandered in foreign lands,
losing your way in the depths.

Time has passed, darkness has descended,
clouds cover the sky.
Your weary body no longer wishes to move,
thorns prick your feet.

Your heart cries out to return home,
but how can you go back now?
"Show me the way," "Show me the way,"
you call out urgently to anyone who might know.

All the friends you had have left,
who remains in this forest?
Oh, the friend of the world is still there,
don't waste your time in vain tears.

Standing at the doorway,
Mother calls out, "Come, grasp my feet."
Dust from the road blinds your eyes,
and you fail to see your Mother.

Where are you, Mother? Where are you?

From where do you call out to me?

Take my hand,
lead me with you to your immortal abode.

What Does It Mean?
This poem reflects on the journey of losing oneself in the illusions of the world and the longing to return home. Tagore speaks of leaving the familiar for foreign lands, only to get lost and face hardships. As time passes and darkness falls, the yearning to return home becomes intense. The cry for guidance and the realization that friends have departed highlight feelings of loneliness and despair. Yet, the divine Mother stands at the doorway, calling out for the return, offering solace and refuge. The poem emphasizes the importance of recognizing and returning to the spiritual home.

How Does It Heal?
"What Have You Done in the Illusion?" offers a powerful message of returning to one's spiritual roots after getting lost in the illusions of the world. It reassures that no matter how lost or weary one feels, the divine presence is always there, waiting to offer solace and guidance. The poem encourages recognizing the call of the divine Mother and the importance of returning to the spiritual home. This understanding fosters

a sense of hope, comfort, and inner peace, helping us navigate life's challenges with renewed strength and clarity.

28. The Day Has Passed, Lord

The day has passed, Lord, in vain—
my heart cries in sorrow.
Life is diminishing every moment—
what has become of this empty life?
How will I show this pale face,
what will I bring when I come near you?
Lord, my fear will vanish,
and I will find hope,
If you call this humble soul.

What Does It Mean?
This poem expresses the sorrow of a life perceived as wasted and the yearning for divine reassurance. Tagore reflects on the passage of time and the diminishing nature of life, filled with regret and a sense of emptiness. The poet questions what he can present before the divine with a face marked by life's struggles. The plea to the Lord to call upon him symbolizes a deep desire for divine intervention, reassurance, and the hope that comes with it.

How Does It Heal?
"The Day Has Passed, Lord" offers a poignant reflection on the feelings of regret and the longing for divine reassurance. The poem acknowledges the sorrow and fear associated with a life perceived as wasted but offers hope in the divine's call.

By seeking the divine's intervention, the poet finds solace and the promise of renewed hope. This message encourages us to turn to our spiritual beliefs for comfort and reassurance, fostering inner peace and resilience in the face of life's challenges.

29. I Am a Traveler

I am a traveler, oh,
No one can hold me back.
The bonds of joy and sorrow are all in vain;
where will this bound home remain behind?

The weight of worldly things pulls me down—
broken, it will scatter and fall.
I am a traveler, oh,
I sing songs with a full heart on my journey.
All the doors of this fortress of the body will open,
all chains of desire will break.

I will cross over good and bad—
traveling from world to world.
I am a traveler, oh,
All burdens will be shed.
The sky calls me towards the distant horizon
with its silent, unknown song.
Morning and evening,
my heart is drawn by the deep sound of someone's flute.
I am a traveler, oh,
I set out not knowing which dawn.

No bird was singing anywhere,
Who knows how much of the night was left?

Only a timeless eye was awake,
watching over the darkness.

What Does It Mean?

This poem speaks to the essence of being a traveler in life, unbound and free. Tagore emphasizes that no one can hold him back, as the bonds of joy and sorrow, and the weight of worldly things, are transient. The imagery of doors opening and chains breaking symbolizes liberation from physical and emotional constraints. The poem expresses a journey beyond good and bad, towards a distant horizon, guided by an unknown, silent song. The timeless eye watching over the darkness suggests a divine presence or eternal consciousness guiding the traveler.

How Does It Heal?

"I Am a Traveler" offers a message of liberation and the transcendence of worldly constraints. It reassures us that the bonds of joy and sorrow are temporary and that true freedom lies in the journey beyond these constraints. By embracing the traveler's spirit, we can find liberation from the burdens of life and be guided by a deeper, timeless consciousness. This perspective fosters resilience, inner peace, and a sense of purpose, helping us navigate life's journey with a full heart and an open spirit.

30. In Joy I Have Seen You

In joy I have seen you,
In sorrow, I have felt you deeply.

Losing you, I have kept you hidden,
Finding you again, I lose myself in the ecstasy of union.

Throughout my life, on the strings of my lyre,
Your touch has struck repeatedly,
That is why, in the varied tunes,
I have felt your touch in my heart.

Now I am no longer afraid,
If this play of life comes to an end here.
In new light and new darkness,
If you take me to a new shore,
You will still be my beloved—
I will recognize you anew once more.

What Does It Mean?
This poem reflects on the poet's enduring connection with the divine or a beloved presence, experienced through both joy and sorrow. Tagore speaks of seeing and feeling this presence deeply in both states. The cycle of losing and finding the divine signifies the ongoing journey of spiritual discovery. The repeated touch on the strings of his lyre

symbolizes life's trials and experiences, through which the divine touch is felt. The poet expresses a readiness to embrace change and new beginnings, confident in recognizing the divine presence in any form or situation.

How Does It Heal?

"In Joy I Have Seen You" offers a comforting message of an enduring divine presence through all of life's experiences. It reassures us that whether in joy or sorrow, the divine is always with us. The poem encourages embracing the journey of losing and finding, as it deepens our connection with the divine. By expressing a fearless acceptance of life's changes and the confidence in recognizing the divine anew, the poem fosters a sense of peace, resilience, and unwavering faith. This perspective helps us navigate life's uncertainties with trust and hope.

31. Eyes Cannot See You

Eyes cannot see you,
yet you remain within the eyes.
Heart cannot know you,
yet you dwell secretly within the heart.

Under the sway of desires,
the mind rushes wildly in all directions like a madman,
Yet you, with unwavering gaze,
are ever awake in my soul,
in sleep and in dreams.

All have left,
those with no one have you,
 they have your love—
Those without shelter,
whose path is their home,
they too find refuge in your abode.

What Does It Mean?
This poem explores the paradox of the unseen and unknowable divine presence that nevertheless resides deeply within us. Tagore speaks of the inability of the eyes to see and the heart to fully comprehend the divine, yet affirms that the divine is ever-present within. The mind, driven by desires, seeks fulfillment wildly, but the divine remains

constant and awake within the soul. The poem highlights the divine's unconditional love and refuge for those who feel abandoned or without shelter.

How Does It Heal?
"Eyes Cannot See You" offers a profound sense of comfort and reassurance by affirming the constant presence of the divine within us. It acknowledges the human struggle with desires and the feeling of abandonment, yet reassures that the divine remains ever-present, loving, and providing refuge. By recognizing this unwavering divine presence, we can find inner peace, resilience, and a sense of belonging. This perspective helps us navigate life's challenges with the assurance that we are never truly alone and always have a refuge in the divine.

32. I Will Not Tell You of My Sorrows

I will not tell you of my sorrows,
for I have forgotten them at your touch.
Whatever you have given me,
O Lord, I have received with joy and contentment.

In this sweet abode of joy,
I dwell in your loving embrace—
Your moon and sun
shower sweet rays upon me.

Every day, new laughter
blooms in the flower garden with each dawn.
Every night, countless stars and planets
gather silently in your celestial assembly.

A mother's affection and a friend's love
continuously pour nectar in countless streams,
The sweet essence of the world's love
immerses me in a river of ambrosia.

Though we are small, we know not death,
for you have given us your fearless refuge.
All grief and pain vanish,
O Lord, at the sight of your feet.

What Does It Mean?

This poem reflects on the transformative power of divine grace and the joy that comes from divine presence. Tagore speaks of forgetting sorrows through the divine touch and finding joy in everything the divine provides. The poem describes the world as a sweet abode of joy filled with divine light and love. It highlights the continuous flow of love and affection from the divine, comparable to the nurturing love of a mother and a friend. The divine presence offers a refuge that transcends the fear of death, where all grief and pain disappear.

How Does It Heal?

"I Will Not Tell You of My Sorrows" offers a message of profound comfort and joy through divine grace. It reassures us that the divine touch can transform sorrows into joy and contentment. By emphasizing the continuous flow of divine love and the nurturing presence of the divine, the poem fosters a sense of peace and security. The assurance that all grief and pain vanish in the presence of the divine helps us navigate life's challenges with resilience and a deep sense of inner joy.

33. Forgive My Weariness, Lord

Forgive my weariness, Lord,
If ever I fall behind on the path.
This trembling heart quivers with fear today—
Forgive this pain, forgive, forgive, forgive, Lord.

Forgive this day, Lord,
If ever I look back.
In the heat of the day, the blazing sun dries the garland on the offering tray—
Forgive this withering, forgive, forgive, forgive, Lord.

What Does It Mean?
This poem is a plea for divine forgiveness and understanding in moments of weakness and weariness. Tagore expresses a humble request for forgiveness if he ever falls behind or looks back on his journey. The trembling heart and the dried garland symbolize the struggles and exhaustion faced along the way. The poet seeks divine compassion and grace to overcome these moments of frailty.

How Does It Heal?
"Forgive My Weariness, Lord" offers a message of seeking and receiving divine forgiveness in times of struggle. It reassures us that it is natural to experience weariness and moments of looking back. By seeking forgiveness and

compassion from the divine, we can find solace and strength to continue our journey. The poem encourages us to acknowledge our vulnerabilities and seek the divine's grace to overcome them, fostering resilience and inner peace.

34. Through the Song

Through the song, when I see the world,
Then I recognize it, then I understand it.

In the language of its light, the sky fills with love,
In every speck of its dust, the ultimate message awakens.

Then it leaves the outside and comes into my inner being,
Then my heart trembles in every blade of its grass.

In the lines of its form, in the flow of its essence,
It loses its boundaries—
Then I see whispers between everyone and me.

What Does It Mean?
This poem reflects the profound connection and understanding of the world through the medium of music. Tagore speaks of recognizing and understanding the world when seen through the lens of a song. The song transforms the sky with love and awakens a deep message in the dust. The divine presence moves from the external to the internal, causing the poet's heart to tremble with a newfound connection. The boundaries between self and others dissolve, revealing an intimate communion with the world.

How Does It Heal?

"Through the Song" offers a message of deep connection and understanding through the transformative power of music. It reassures us that by engaging with the world through a creative and soulful medium, we can gain profound insights and a sense of unity. The poem encourages us to find and nurture these connections within ourselves, fostering a sense of love, understanding, and inner peace. This perspective helps us appreciate the beauty and unity in the world, offering solace and a deeper sense of belonging.

35. The Traveler Thought

The traveler thought—their torch flames,
Are not just a mirage of the twilight.

They believed—these flames,
Would burn brightly like the stars of the northern sky,
Held in the immortal southern hand.

They imagined that with the fierce power of these flames,
The fortresses of the night would burn,
Breaking through the locked doors of darkness,
They would seize the treasures of eternity;
Making the earth their servant of enjoyment.

The bells ring, the bells ring.
Suddenly, they are startled to find they were blind in their slumber.
Oh, they were seeing themselves in a dream,
Dressed as kings on the throne of the enchanted palace;
As if they had looted the universe of Maheshwar with a loud laugh.

In the void, the new sun rises.

What Does It Mean?

This poem explores the dreams and illusions of power and conquest. Tagore describes how travelers, inspired by their torch flames, believe they can conquer the darkness and seize the treasures of eternity. However, the ringing bells awaken them from their slumber, revealing that their visions of grandeur were mere dreams. The poem concludes with the awakening of a new sun, symbolizing a new beginning or enlightenment after the illusions have faded.

How Does It Heal?

"The Traveler Thought" offers a reflection on the illusions of power and the humbling realization that often follows. It reassures us that while dreams of grandeur and conquest may be enticing, true enlightenment comes from awakening to reality. The poem encourages us to embrace humility and recognize the transient nature of such illusions. This perspective fosters a sense of inner peace and acceptance, helping us navigate life's aspirations and setbacks with a balanced outlook.

36. One Silent Night

One silent night,
Sleepless,
In the sway of emotions,
With bowed head,
In tears,
You gently kissed my palm and said—

"If you go far away,
Endlessly,
The weight of emptiness
Will turn my world
Into a barren desert.

The vast weariness of the sky
Will take all peace
From my heart—
Joyless, lightless,
A silent sorrow
Worse than death.

What Does It Mean?
This poem captures a poignant moment of deep emotional connection and vulnerability. Tagore describes a sleepless night filled with emotional turmoil, where someone expresses their profound sorrow and fear of losing the poet.

The act of gently kissing the poet's palm while speaking conveys intense love and the fear that separation would bring unbearable emptiness and desolation, turning their world into a barren wasteland and taking away all peace and joy.

How Does It Heal?

"One Silent Night" offers a deep reflection on the pain of separation and the profound impact it can have on one's emotional state. The poem reassures us that such feelings of sorrow and fear are part of the human experience, validating our emotions. By expressing these deep emotions, the poem helps us process and understand the weight of such feelings, fostering empathy and connection. This understanding can bring comfort and healing, reminding us of the importance of emotional bonds and the shared human experience of love and loss.

37. Play Me

Play me,
Play me in the tune that brings the morning light.

The tune that fills wordless songs,
In the fresh breath of a child's life,
In a mother's smile as she gazes at her baby—
Play me in that tune.

Adorn me,
Adorn me in the way you dress the earth's dust.

In the rhythm of the evening jasmine,
With its secret fragrance,
In the adornment that forgets itself in joy—
Adorn me in that way.

What Does It Mean?
This poem expresses a deep longing to be in harmony with the beauty and essence of life. Tagore asks to be played in the same tune that brings the morning light, symbolizing new beginnings and innocence. He wants to be adorned in the way that nature itself is adorned, with the pure and secret joy that comes from within. The imagery of a child's breath, a mother's smile, and the evening jasmine evokes a sense of purity, joy, and inner beauty.

How Does It Heal?

"Play Me" offers a message of longing for harmony and beauty in life. It reassures us that by aligning ourselves with the natural rhythms and simple joys of life, we can find peace and fulfillment. The poem encourages us to seek out and cherish the innocent and pure moments, fostering a sense of inner joy and harmony. This perspective helps us appreciate the small beauties of life and find solace in the natural, joyful rhythms around us.

Section 2: Healing and Tagore

1. Why Does Poetry Heal

Poetry has a unique ability to heal the human spirit. Here are several reasons why:

1. **Mirror for Self-Reflection**
    - **Explanation**: Poetry often mirrors our own thoughts and emotions, allowing us to see ourselves more clearly.
    - **Healing Power**: By reflecting on the themes and emotions in a poem, we can gain insights into our own lives, fostering self-awareness and growth.

2. **Diagnose Strengths and Weaknesses**
    - **Explanation**: Poetry can help us identify our strengths and weaknesses, much like a doctor diagnosing a patient.
    - **Healing Power**: Understanding our capabilities and areas for improvement enables us to address our flaws and leverage our strengths, promoting personal development.

3. **Healing, Soothing Words**
    - **Explanation**: The rhythmic and melodic nature of poetry can be calming and soothing.

- **Healing Power**: Gentle, comforting words can reduce stress and anxiety, creating a sense of peace and well-being.

4. **Provides Moral Support and Encouragement**
   - **Explanation**: Poetry often contains messages of encouragement and moral support.
   - **Healing Power**: Inspirational verses can uplift our spirits, motivate us to persevere, and provide comfort during difficult times.

5. **Provides Hope and Shows Light**
   - **Explanation**: Many poems offer hope and illuminate paths through dark times.
   - **Healing Power**: By presenting hopeful perspectives, poetry helps us see beyond our current struggles, fostering resilience and optimism.

6. **Acts as a Positive Hiding Place from Pain**
   - **Explanation**: Engaging with poetry can provide a temporary escape from the pain and challenges of life.
   - **Healing Power**: This mental retreat allows us to recover and recharge, offering a safe space to process our emotions.

7. **Acts as Surrogate Meditations**
    - **Explanation**: Reading or reciting poetry can mimic the effects of meditation, bringing focus and tranquility.
    - **Healing Power**: This meditative quality helps calm the mind, reduce stress, and promote emotional balance.

8. **Facilitates Emotional Expression**
    - **Explanation**: Poetry provides a structured way to express complex emotions that might be difficult to articulate otherwise.
    - **Healing Power**: Expressing emotions through poetry can be cathartic, helping to release pent-up feelings and leading to emotional relief.

9. **Enhances Empathy and Connection**
    - **Explanation**: Poetry often explores universal themes and shared human experiences.
    - **Healing Power**: This connection fosters empathy, helping us feel understood and less isolated in our struggles.

10. **Promotes Mindfulness**
    - **Explanation**: The focus required to read and interpret poetry encourages mindfulness and present-moment awareness.

- **Healing Power**: Practicing mindfulness through poetry can reduce stress, enhance mental clarity, and improve overall well-being.

11. **Inspires Creativity and Imagination**
    - **Explanation**: Poetry stimulates the imagination and encourages creative thinking.
    - **Healing Power**: Engaging in creative activities has been shown to improve mental health, providing an outlet for expression and problem-solving.

Poetry serves as a powerful tool for personal and emotional well-being, guiding us through self-reflection, providing comfort, and fostering a deeper understanding of ourselves and the world around us.

2. Healing Attributes of Humanity

Based on the works of Rumi, Hafiz, Kabir, and Tagore, the following attributes are essential for healing ourselves:

Devotion to the Divine
Patience
Forgiveness
Tolerance
Self-Awareness
Humility
Compassion
Love
Resilience
Acceptance
Gratitude
Why These Attributes Heal

Devotion to the Divine

Explanation: Devotion to the divine provides a sense of security and purpose. Just as a child finds comfort and stops crying when assured of their mother's presence, knowing that a higher power is there to protect and guide us is profoundly liberating. It offers a sense of peace and removes the burden of fear and uncertainty.

Healing Power: This devotion creates a sanctuary for the soul, fostering inner peace and resilience. It helps individuals cope with life's challenges by placing trust in something greater than themselves.

Patience

Explanation: Patience allows individuals to endure difficult situations with grace and calm. It acknowledges that everything happens in its own time and teaches us to wait without anxiety or frustration.

Healing Power: By cultivating patience, we reduce stress and anxiety, allowing the healing process to unfold naturally. It promotes mental and emotional stability.

Forgiveness

Explanation: Forgiveness involves letting go of grudges and resentment, freeing oneself from the negative emotions that weigh us down. It is a conscious decision to release feelings of anger and vengeance.

Healing Power: Forgiveness heals by removing the toxic emotions that hinder emotional and psychological well-being. It fosters inner peace and improves relationships.

Tolerance

Explanation: Tolerance is the ability to accept and respect differences, whether in beliefs, behaviors, or lifestyles. It encourages an open mind and a non-judgmental attitude.

Healing Power: Tolerance reduces conflicts and promotes harmony. It allows for peaceful coexistence and mutual respect, which are essential for a healthy community and personal peace.

Self-Awareness

Explanation: Self-awareness involves understanding one's thoughts, emotions, and behaviors. It is the foundation of personal growth and development.

Healing Power: By being self-aware, individuals can identify the root causes of their pain and take proactive steps to address them. It leads to better emotional regulation and decision-making.

Humility

Explanation: Humility is recognizing our limitations and being open to learning from others. It involves acknowledging that we are not superior to anyone else.

Healing Power: Humility fosters a sense of community and connection. It opens the door to growth and learning, reducing feelings of isolation and arrogance that can harm relationships.

Compassion

Explanation: Compassion is the ability to empathize with others' suffering and take action to alleviate it. It is rooted in kindness and a genuine concern for others.

Healing Power: Compassion promotes positive social interactions and support systems. It helps individuals feel understood and cared for, which is vital for emotional healing.

Love

Explanation: Love is a profound and selfless affection towards others. It can manifest as romantic love, familial love, or universal love for all beings.

Healing Power: Love provides emotional support and security. It nurtures the soul and fosters a sense of belonging and connection, essential for overall well-being.

Resilience

Explanation: Resilience is the ability to bounce back from adversity. It involves adaptability and perseverance in the face of challenges.

Healing Power: Resilience helps individuals cope with stress and recover from setbacks. It fosters a positive outlook and encourages continuous personal growth.

Acceptance

Explanation: Acceptance involves recognizing and embracing reality as it is, without resisting or denying it. It is about finding peace with circumstances we cannot change.

Healing Power: Acceptance reduces inner conflict and promotes peace of mind. It helps individuals move forward and focus on what they can control, fostering emotional stability.

Gratitude

Explanation: Gratitude is the practice of acknowledging and appreciating the good things in life. It shifts focus from what is lacking to what is abundant.

Healing Power: Gratitude enhances overall happiness and well-being. It reduces negative emotions and fosters a positive outlook, which is beneficial for mental health.

These attributes, as expressed through the wisdom of Tagore, provide a comprehensive guide for emotional and spiritual healing. By embracing these qualities, individuals can cultivate a more fulfilling, peaceful, and resilient life.

3. Step by Step Guide: Healing Through Poetry

Healing through poetry is a profound journey of spiritual and emotional growth. Poetry, with its rich symbolism and deep spiritual insights, provides a path to healing by guiding individuals towards inner peace and divine connection.

Step 1: Find the Right Environment
Explanation: Create a serene and comfortable space where you can read and reflect on poetry without distractions.

Practice: Choose a quiet room, light a candle or incense, and ensure you have a comfortable place to sit.

Step 2: Select Your Poems
Explanation: Choose poems that resonate with your current emotional or spiritual state. Poetry is diverse and can address various aspects of the human experience.

Practice: Begin with well-known poems by Tagore focusing on themes of love, divine connection, and inner peace.

Step 3: Read Slowly and Reflect
Explanation: Poetry is meant to be savored. Read slowly to fully absorb the meanings and emotions conveyed in the verses.

Practice: Read each poem multiple times. Pause after each line to reflect on its significance and how it relates to your own life.

Step 4: Journal Your Thoughts
Explanation: Writing down your reflections can deepen your understanding and provide a record of your emotional and spiritual journey.

Practice: After reading each poem, journal your thoughts, feelings, and any insights gained. Note how the poem speaks to your current state of being.

Step 5: Meditate on Key Phrases
Explanation: Meditation helps internalize the wisdom of the poetry and fosters a deeper connection with the divine.

Practice: Choose a key phrase or line from the poem. Sit quietly, close your eyes, and repeat the phrase silently. Focus on its meaning and let it permeate your mind and heart.

Step 6: Engage in Contemplative Practices
Explanation: Contemplative practices such as prayer, chanting, or breathing exercises can enhance the healing process.

Practice: Integrate contemplative practices into your reading sessions. For example, recite a poem as a prayer or incorporate rhythmic breathing while reflecting on the verses.

Step 7: Discuss with Others

Explanation: Sharing your experiences and insights with others can provide new perspectives and foster a sense of community.

Practice: Join a poetry group or find a partner with whom you can discuss the poems. Share your interpretations and listen to theirs, enhancing your understanding.

Step 8: Apply the Wisdom in Daily Life

Explanation: The ultimate goal of healing through poetry is to integrate its wisdom into your everyday actions and thoughts.

Practice: Reflect on how the lessons from the poems can be applied to your daily life. Practice compassion, patience, and love as inspired by the poetry.

3. Tagore and the Bhagavad Gita

While it is not definitively known if Tagore formally studied the Bhagavad Gita, his writings often reflect its profound wisdom and themes. The Bhagavad Gita, a sacred Hindu scripture, explores concepts of duty, devotion, and the nature of reality. Tagore's poems and songs frequently mirror these themes, suggesting a deep resonance with the teachings of the Gita. Below, we explore some key concepts from the Bhagavad Gita and their reflection in Tagore's works.

1. The Concept of Duty (Dharma)
Bhagavad Gita:

In the Bhagavad Gita, Lord Krishna emphasizes the importance of performing one's duty without attachment to the results. This is encapsulated in the verse:

"You have the right to perform your duty, but not to the fruits of your actions." (Bhagavad Gita 2:47)

Tagore:

Tagore's poem "Ekla Chalo Re" (If They Answer Not to Thy Call, Walk Alone) embodies this spirit of duty and perseverance:

"If no one heeds your call, then walk alone, walk alone."

This reflects the Gita's message of steadfastly performing one's duty regardless of external support or recognition.

2. The Nature of the Self
Bhagavad Gita:
The Gita speaks about the eternal nature of the soul, which is beyond birth and death:

"The soul is neither born, and nor does it die... It is not slain when the body is slain." (Bhagavad Gita 2:20)

Tagore:
In Tagore's "Gitanjali," the concept of the eternal soul is echoed:

"I am a poet. I will continue to exist through my songs even after I die."

Tagore's belief in the immortality of the soul and the enduring nature of his art parallels the Gita's teachings on the eternal self.

3. Detachment and Surrender
Bhagavad Gita:
Krishna advises Arjuna to surrender all actions to the divine and remain detached from the outcomes:

"Surrender all actions to Me, with your mind fixed on the Self, free from desire and ego." (Bhagavad Gita 3:30)

Tagore:
Tagore's song "Jodi Tor Dak Shune Keu Na Ase Tobe Ekla Cholo Re" (If No One Responds to Your Call, Then Go On Alone) also promotes the idea of acting with detachment and inner resolve:

"If they do not hold up the light, then hold up your light alone."

This encourages pursuing one's path with inner strength and detachment from external validation.

4. The Unity of Life
Bhagavad Gita:
The Gita teaches the unity of all life and the presence of the divine in every being:

"The one who sees the same divine presence in all beings, truly sees." (Bhagavad Gita 6:29)

Tagore:
In "Gitanjali," Tagore often speaks of the divine presence in all aspects of life:

"Where the mind is led forward by thee into ever-widening thought and action—Into that heaven of freedom, my Father, let my country awake."

This reflects the Gita's vision of seeing the divine in all and striving for a unity of purpose.

5. The Importance of Devotion (Bhakti)
Bhagavad Gita:
Krishna emphasizes the power of devotion in attaining spiritual liberation:

"Whoever offers Me with love and devotion a leaf, a flower, fruit, or water, I accept that offering." (Bhagavad Gita 9:26)

Tagore:
Tagore's devotional songs express deep love and surrender to the divine, such as in "Gitanjali":

"I am here to sing thee songs. In this hall of thine I have a corner seat."

Tagore's devotion and his expression of love through his art resonate with the Gita's teachings on bhakti.

Conclusion

While there is no concrete evidence that Tagore studied the Bhagavad Gita formally, his writings and songs reflect its themes profoundly. Through his exploration of duty, the nature of the self, detachment, the unity of life, and devotion, Tagore's works resonate with the timeless wisdom of the Gita.

3. Healing vs Personal Identity

As a practicing doctor and an author, I have observed a profound connection between personal identity and the process of healing. The more fundamental and unified your sense of identity, the easier it becomes to heal. Conversely, when you carry fragmented or multiple secondary and tertiary identities, you are more prone to internal conflict and negative emotions such as hatred, anger, and jealousy, which can impede healing.

Fundamental Identity and Healing
When your identity is rooted in fundamental aspects like being human or being a living being, it simplifies your sense of self. This foundational identity is less susceptible to the fluctuations and stressors of external circumstances, allowing for a more stable and resilient sense of self. This stability promotes mental and emotional well-being, which is essential for the healing process.

Key Points:
Unified Identity: A single, cohesive identity reduces internal conflict and stress.

Resilience: A stable sense of self helps in coping with life's challenges, fostering resilience.

Emotional Stability: Fundamental identities are less likely to be affected by external validation or criticism, leading to emotional stability.

Fragmented Identities and Suffering

When individuals identify strongly with multiple roles or characteristics (e.g., professional titles, social status, affiliations), they often experience fragmentation of the self. This fragmentation can lead to internal conflicts and a heightened sensitivity to external circumstances, which may trigger negative emotions and impede the healing process.

Key Points:
Internal Conflict: Multiple identities can lead to conflicting desires and values, causing internal turmoil.

Sensitivity to External Factors: Fragmented identities often rely on external validation, making individuals more vulnerable to negative emotions.

Increased Suffering: Negative emotions like anger, jealousy, and hatred are more prevalent, complicating the healing process.

Simplifying Identity for Better Healing

By simplifying your identity to its most fundamental aspects, such as identifying primarily as a human or a living being, you can reduce the likelihood of experiencing negative emotions that hinder healing. This approach fosters a sense of unity and connection with all life, promoting compassion, understanding, and emotional balance.

Benefits:
Less Anger and Jealousy: A simplified identity reduces the sources of comparison and competition, leading to fewer negative emotions.

Greater Compassion: Identifying with the fundamental aspects of life fosters a sense of connection with others, enhancing compassion and empathy.

Enhanced Healing: Emotional balance and reduced stress levels create a conducive environment for physical and mental healing.

Practical Steps to Simplify Identity
Mindfulness Practices: Engage in mindfulness and meditation to connect with your fundamental self.

Reflect on Core Values: Identify and embrace core values that define you as a human being, rather than external labels.

Practice Compassion: Cultivate compassion for yourself and others, focusing on shared human experiences.

Conclusion

Understanding the relationship between personal identity and healing is crucial for achieving emotional and physical well-being. By simplifying your identity to its most fundamental aspects, you can reduce internal conflicts and negative emotions, thereby creating a more conducive environment for healing.

4. Science vs Religion: Discord or Symphony?

The longstanding debate between science and religion often frames these domains as inherently at odds. However, this perspective overlooks the complementary strengths each brings to the human experience. Science equips us with tangible results and practical knowledge, enhancing our ability to understand and manipulate the physical world. Religion, when understood as a structured practice cultivating virtues like love, compassion, kindness, forgiveness, gratitude, and serenity, enriches our inner lives, fostering peace and happiness.

The Strengths of Science
Science offers a methodical approach to understanding the natural world. Through observation, experimentation, and evidence-based conclusions, science provides us with concrete tools and knowledge. It empowers us to solve problems, innovate, and improve our quality of life.

Key Benefits:
Tangible Results: Scientific discoveries lead to technological advancements, medical breakthroughs, and a deeper understanding of the universe.

Empowerment: Knowledge gained from science enhances our ability to address challenges and create solutions.

Progress: Science drives progress in numerous fields, contributing to societal development and well-being.

The Virtues of Religion

Religion, when focused on nurturing virtues, offers intangible but profound benefits. Practices that promote love, compassion, kindness, forgiveness, gratitude, and serenity create a foundation for a fulfilling and harmonious life. These virtues help us build meaningful relationships, find inner peace, and cultivate a sense of purpose.

Key Benefits:

Inner Peace: Religious practices can lead to a peaceful and contented state of mind.

Moral Guidance: Religion provides a moral framework that encourages ethical behavior and social harmony.

Community and Support: Religious communities offer social support, fostering a sense of belonging and mutual care.

Complementary Domains

Rather than viewing science and religion as discordant, it is more constructive to see them as complementary. Science addresses the external, material aspects of life, while religion nurtures the internal, spiritual dimensions. Together, they provide a holistic approach to human well-being.

Symphony of Science and Religion:
Holistic Understanding: Science explains the "how" of the universe, while religion addresses the "why."

Enhanced Well-being: Combining scientific knowledge with religious virtues leads to a balanced, fulfilling life.

Mutual Enrichment: Science can inform religious practices, while religious values can guide the ethical use of scientific advancements.

Caveat: Defining Religion

It is crucial to define what we mean by religion. For the purposes of this discussion, religion is understood as a structured practice that cultivates positive virtues. Practices that promote intolerance, hatred, or division are not considered true religion but rather distortions that can lead to harm.

Key Considerations:
Positive Virtues: True religion fosters love, compassion, kindness, forgiveness, gratitude, and serenity.
Avoiding Extremism: Practices that incite violence or hatred contradict the essence of true religion.

Informed Debate: When engaging in discussions about science vs. religion, it is essential to clarify these definitions to avoid misunderstandings and promote constructive dialogue.

Conclusion

Viewing science and religion as complementary rather than contradictory allows for a more nuanced and holistic understanding of the human experience. Science empowers us with knowledge and practical tools, while religion nurtures our inner virtues and provides moral guidance. By embracing both, we can achieve a balanced and harmonious life. It is essential to define religion in terms of practices that genuinely promote positive virtues, avoiding those that lead to division and harm.

5. Tagore as a Healer, Humanist, and Proponent of Human Identity

Rabindranath Tagore, the esteemed poet, philosopher, and Nobel laureate, stands out as a healer, humanist, and advocate for the fundamental identity of being human. His works transcend mere literary excellence, offering profound insights into the human condition and fostering a sense of unity and compassion among people. Tagore's emphasis on the primary identity of being human over other fragmented identities positions him as a timeless figure whose teachings continue to resonate with contemporary issues.

Tagore as a Healer

Tagore's poetry and writings often serve as a balm for the soul, addressing the deep emotional and spiritual needs of individuals. His exploration of universal themes like love, sorrow, joy, and the quest for meaning provides comfort and guidance to those in distress.

Healing Through Poetry:

Emotional Resonance: Tagore's verses capture the subtleties of human emotions, offering solace and understanding to readers.

Spiritual Insight: His works frequently delve into spiritual reflections, encouraging readers to find peace and purpose within themselves.

Unity and Compassion: By promoting a sense of connectedness among all beings, Tagore's writings foster a compassionate worldview that heals societal rifts.
Example:

In his poem "Gitanjali," Tagore writes:
"Let me not pray to be sheltered from dangers, but to be fearless in facing them. Let me not beg for the stilling of my pain, but for the heart to conquer it."

This reflects his approach to healing, encouraging resilience and inner strength.

Tagore as a Humanist
Tagore's humanism is evident in his unwavering belief in the potential and dignity of every individual. He championed education, cultural exchange, and social reform, believing in the inherent goodness and creativity of people.

Humanist Values:
Universal Brotherhood: Tagore advocated for a global sense of community, transcending national and cultural boundaries.

Educational Reform: He founded Visva-Bharati University, emphasizing holistic education that nurtures both intellect and spirit.

Social Justice: His writings often critique social inequalities and call for justice and fairness.

Example:
In his essay "Crisis in Civilization," Tagore laments the materialistic tendencies of modern society and underscores the importance of spiritual and moral development:
"We may become powerful by knowledge, but we attain fullness by sympathy."

Proponent of Human Identity
Tagore's emphasis on the primary identity of being human challenges the divisive tendencies of fragmented identities based on race, religion, nationality, or social status. He believed that recognizing our shared humanity is key to overcoming conflict and fostering peace.

Primary Identity as Human:
Beyond Fragmentation: Tagore urged people to see beyond secondary identities and embrace the fundamental identity of being human.

Inclusive Philosophy: His inclusive philosophy promotes acceptance, understanding, and unity.

Peace and Harmony: By prioritizing human identity, Tagore's teachings encourage a harmonious coexistence, free from prejudice and division.

Example:
In his poem "The Child," Tagore writes:
"On the seashore of endless worlds, children meet. The infinite sky is motionless overhead, and the restless water is boisterous. On the seashore of endless worlds, the children meet with shouts and dances."

This metaphor of children meeting without prejudice underscores his vision of a unified human identity.

Conclusion
Rabindranath Tagore's writings offer emotional and spiritual healing, advocate for human dignity and potential, and promote a universal identity that transcends divisive boundaries. By embracing Tagore's teachings, we can cultivate a more compassionate, just, and harmonious world, rooted in the recognition of our shared humanity.

Author's Bio

Dr. Arun Maji is a practicing physician based in Sydney. As a former military doctor in many battlefields around the world, he has seen it all—human cry amidst war, and human hope and resilience even in unexpected places. He has lived in the cold Himalayan caves with a monkey on his lap! Yes, what a way to seek enlightenment!

When not immersed in the practice of medicine, he dedicates his time to reading and writing on a diverse array of subjects. Dr. Maji is a firm believer in the richness of human experience and the importance of trying everything life has to offer. This philosophy is reflected in his celebration of diverse cultures and beliefs, and it permeates his varied literary pursuits.

Shakespearean Adaptations:
William Shakespeare's A Midsummer Night's Dream: Adaptation - Simple, Poetic, Elegant
Shakespeare's Romeo And Juliet: For Teens And Adults
Shakespeare's The Comedy Of Errors: A Tale Of Mistaken Identities For Children And Adults
Shakespeare's Twelfth Night: Romantic Comedy For Children And Adults
William Shakespeare's Macbeth: Adaptation - Simple, Poetic, Elegant
Shakespeare's King Lear: Easy, Poetic, Elegant
Shakespeare's The Tempest: Magically Romantic Comedy For Children And Adults

Shakepeare's Antony And Cleopatra: For Students And Adults
Shakespeare's Julius Caesar: Easy For Students And Adults
Shakespeare's Othello: Easy Play For Kids, Teens, And All
Shakespeare's Much Ado About Nothing: Romantic Comedy For Children And Adults
Romeo And Juliet Of The Ganges: An Immortal Love Story Based On Shakespeare
King Who Begged from His Daughters: Based on Shakespeare

Novels, Stories, Inspiring Stories:
Warrior Arjuna: Echo Of Hercules, Achilles, And David
Draupadi: The Queen Of Fire
Princess Amba: Thirsty For Revenge
Karna: The Tragic Hero Of India
Kunti: Cry Of A Queen
Arjuna: The Immortal Warrior
Abhimanyu: Prince Who Learnt War Strategy In His Mother's Womb
Cleopatra: The Envy Of Rome
Shakuntala: The Abandoned Queen
The Haunted King: Ajatashatru
Krishna: The Divine Strategist
Leadership: Learn It From Krishna
Servant King: Vow Of Chandra And Rohini
Bhishma: Vow Unto Death
Art Of Living: Yaksha Yudhisthira Dialogue
War: Within & Outside
The Veiled Woman: A Tale Of Love, Passion, Desire, And Mystery
Rise From Ashes: A Romance Novel That Inspires

the Conflicted Heart
Rise Of India: Boosts And Barriers
Prince Bharata: The Father of India
PARASHURAMA: Fury of A Sage Warrior
Return from Death: Beating Cancer and Beyond
Rise Like Phoenix: Inspiration from A Bereaved Mother

Poetry Books:
30 Jewels: Heal Through Rumi
30 Jewels: Best of Shakespeare
30 Jewels: Heal Through Tagore
Healing Poetry: 30 Jewels
The Inferno: Poetry Of Passion
The Fire: Love & Ruin
Love, Fire, Earth
Song Of The Soul
Prem Porinoy Prithibi
Malavika: Fire And Ashes

Self-Help Books (Women's Health):
Building A Strong Baby: Doctor's Pregnancy Guide
Motherhood: The Ultimate Sacrifice
Cosmic Love: Secrets Of Lasting Passion

Self-Help Books (Mental Health, Personal Transformation):
Did Buddha Suffer Depression?: A Doctor's Guide To Mental Health
Science vs Bhagavad Gita: On Healing
Secret Whisper: Stop! Listen To The Sun, Moon, And River
Win Over Suffering: Science, Philosophy, Spirituality

Young Mind Beautiful Mind: Holistic Handbook On Teen's Health

Relationship Bible: Holistic Relationship Workbook For Men And Women

Heal Yourself: Ancient Wisdom For Modern Ailments

Win Over Childhood Obesity: Guide For Children, Parents, Teachers, And Health Professionals

Mind Game: Beyond Grey Matter

Love: Known battlefield, Unknown War

Printed in Great Britain
by Amazon